THREADS OF BOHEMIA

THREADS OF BOHEMIA

Carlin W. Allen

COPYRIGHT DISCLAIMER

The works presented in this book are based off of my own personal memories, told from my perspective, and I have tried to represent events as faithfully as possible. Some scenarios presented or described in this book are fictitious. Any similarity to actual persons, living or dead, is coincidental.

Copyright © 2024 Carlin W. Allen

All rights reserved. No part of this book may be reproduced or used in any manner without the prior written permission of the copyright owner, except for the use of brief quotations in a book review.

To request permissions, please contact the publisher at cwapoetry@pm.me

Instagram: @cwapoetry
Threads: @cwapoetry

AUTHOR'S BOOKS

Hues of Humanity: A Poetry Collection

Threads of Bohemia: Another Poetry Collection

This collection of poetry explores, from a Bohemian perspective, the elements of the human spirit which make life worth living— as told through the subjective, but relatable lens of my own personal experiences.

TABLE OF CONTENTS

CHAPTER ONE: AUTHENTICITY ---------------- **11**

CHAPTER TWO: LIBERATION -------------------- **33**

CHAPTER THREE: BEAUTY ----------------------- **51**

CHAPTER FOUR: IMAGINATION ---------------- **69**

CHAPTER FIVE: TRUE LOVE ---------------------- **83**

Dedicated to the lovers, the dreamers, and the courageous, in the many, many forms they take.

CHAPTER ONE: AUTHENTICITY

"VERITY"

Listlessly, she glances
towards firmament.
Light, as shadow, dances,
equal in measurement,
as her mild temperament…

Visage, peachy and fair,
enrapturing coy fools
with resplendent flair,
capturing with dual
causality as fuel…

Golden hair, fluid and smooth,
shifting to aptly please,
comfort and sweetly soothe,
shrifting by deadly squeeze
those unable to appease…

Rigid eyes, sharp and stern,
ever-cruel, ever-feared.
Untelling, yet well-learned,
sagacious and unpeered
amongst e'en those endeared…

Wishlessly, she judges,
discerning lie from fact,
lacking both praise, grudges,
ruling with stark impact.
Adamantine. Uncracked.

"I'M SORRY"

For the lies I tell myself,
about a soul so pure,
wanting the kind of love that endures,
when I feel I've been put on the shelf.
I'm sorry.

For the way I display
the anger I cannot control,
when I really just want you to hold,
when my head and heart fill with dismay.
I'm sorry.

Sorry for the pain
I cannot contain,
from a time I feigned
content and joy.
Sorry I'm insane,
when things get mundane,
and for the text chains.

I'm still just a boy,
who's only learned how to worry.
So, I'm sorry.

For the lack of trust in us.
Though love still shimmers in your eyes,
My scarred mind obscures truth, as I
defile diamonds with dregs of dust.
I'm sorry.

For demons I hide inside
the fake laughs and feeble smiles,
grown in fear and doubt, while
what I need is your gentle light.
I'm sorry.

Sorry for each night
we would yell and fight,
and I'd push you right
out the door.
Sorry I'm not bright,

but dark with fogged fright.

Wish I could, I might
hold you just once more,
to show my real love, and not need to say…
I'm sorry.

"WOEFUL PLEA"

Brightly the sun does shine.
But his warmth I can't feel.
The clear morning is mine,
yet lacks any appeal.
The wind speaks words divine,
whispering cosmic signs,
but I can't seem to heal
'cause these woes are too real.

I reflect with all my might,
and cleanse in holy streams.
Yet I can't find your light.
Nothing is as it seems.
Each and every night
do we argue and fight,
losing sight of our dreams,
hope ripping at the seams.

Still, as this heart beats yet,
let it not speak of regret.
Let it not bleed 'til dead.
Let grow the seeds we've fed.
Recall flames from our youth.
Forget blame for deeds uncouth.
Doubt and shame do not choose.
Play no games, we won't lose.

"MOM'S DAY"

I'm new and open my bright eyes
Meeting your wide but gentle smile
And holding tightly your thumb

You comfort me each time I cry
I was late, waded for a while
Haven't learned yet how to hum

The long journey has just begun
But I know with you by my side
There is nothing I can't do

This is the best Mom's Day with you…

Kindergarten's here, now I'm five
I'm so scared that I wet my pants
You bring me lunch everyday

You teach me how to share and give
That everyone deserves a chance
Love our pony ride pulling hay

Don't know how long I'll feel this way
Or how long my eyes can stay wide
But I love when we sing Xanadu

Making the best Mom's Day with you…

Ten years it took to get to here
Play G.I. Joe, like She-Ra's tools
We go camping for the first time

You teach me there's nothing to fear
Being different, making my own rules
Playing my own tunes on wind chimes

I hear you fighting with Esther
I run away, cry while I hide

But I'm glad I'm found, held by you

On the very best Mom's Day with you…

I'm fifteen, don't know how I feel
Or even which way I should go
I try to do and be what's right

Other boys like to mock, make me squeal
You enroll me in Kajukenbo
To show them I know how to fight

You teach me to be confident
Even when I am scared inside
To never quit, to see things through

I shared the best Mom's Day with you…

"FOUR"

I won't lie.
This world is harsh, evil and cruel.
It will leave you hungry, and cold,
feeling thoughtlessly controlled.
Empty inside. Lost with no fuel.

I won't lie, too.
Others will look down on you.
They will throw salt in your eyes,
tell you how much they despise
everything you hold dearly true.

They will laugh.
You will cry.
They'll call you daft.
But when you want to die,
just picture my warm smile,
and remember that I
would fly a hundred thousand miles

to kiss all of your tears dry.
Because you're a beautiful boon.
And I love you to the moon.

I won't lie.
The world is a hard place.
It can be angry and mean.
It will push you to the brink,
and take shots at your face.

I won't lie to you.
Others will leave you hurt and scarred.
Make you believe you are worthless,
telling you suck and are a mess.
Make you feel gutted, shamed and marred.

They'll be tough.
They'll have lied.
Make you think you're not enough.
But when you want to hide, just picture my warm eyes,
And remember that I

will never truly say goodbye.

I'll stay by you through each night.

You're never really alone, it's true!

Because I will always love you.

"THE TRAVELER AND THE SPARROW"

A traveler through storm did walk,
finding shelter beneath bent bough.
Weary from torrential onslaught,
and lost from all main roads somehow,
bed he made to rest his head…

Next day, when rains and clouds had passed,
and the glorious dawn did rise,
the man beheld, over breakfast,
wounded sparrow with blinded eyes,
wing broken and no voice to sing…

Taking pity on newfound charge,
despite need to search for paths home,
grinding wild nuts and berries large,
and making songs of well-known poems,
fed he the bird and wrapped her head…

Through many weeks of sleet and snow,
took he sparrow to mountaintop,
to listen to fellow sparrows
singing of the morning's dewdrops,
warm sun to follow bitter storm…

At winter's end, did they depart.
Sparrow ahead on mended wing,
of dewdrop hills and chimney hearths
upon hidden pathways, she'd sing,
'til, lo! They found his window's sill!

Weeping with joy, his kin received
the lost and weary nomad man,
and for a minute he believed
their path was paved by guiding hand,
through bird, and song, and love for dew…

Each spring, therefrom, sparrow returned,
with her family's young in tow,
giving thanks for the lessons learned,

by cheerful chirps near his window—
'Song of the Ever-Rising Dawn.'

For, no matter how bleak storms be,
warm sun rises every morn,
just beyond where the eyes can see,
to bring respite in kindness born
through fellowed love—in we—in you.

"MY YOUTH"

I was buried at four years old,
covered in snow and cold.
Taught to do as I was told.
Taught I would always be wrong.

At seven, I was just a pain,
snubbed by those who wouldn't deign
to care enough to explain,
to dare enough to speak in song.

By ten, I'd committed crimes,
stealing nickels and dimes
to play chaotic wind chimes,
to play Carnegie before long.

Blissfully lost at thirteen,
wild, reckless and carefree.
My first drink, or two, or three.
My first time feeling like I belong.

At sixteen, felt my first crush,
dreaming of diamonds with my brush.
Dreaming of love's thrilling rush,
then cried for Elizabeth Hong.

By nineteen, I found my voice,
learned to quiet the noise.
Learned to diet with poise.
And secretly dance along.

Twenty-one, broke some hearts.
Had mine slowly torn apart.
Found true friends at Kwik-E-Mart
Found myself in the throng.

Twenty-five fleeting years
brought love, and pain, and tears.
Taught truth unfeigned through cheers,
self-relevance in ping pong,
and value in the never-long.

"FOR A SPELL"

Swiftly the sands of time flow.
Twenty years have come and gone,
without so much as a glow,
or a sparkle, or great bon
fire, just like we used to do…

The wheels of life keep turning.
Our feet shuffle, on and on.
Away from youthful yearning,
our escapades through the dawn,
going which way the wind blew…

But if you caught sight of me,
would you even invite me
for a spell of that lightning?
And would you recognize me?

Would we choose the right kind of speech,
and fly high like kites on the reef,

or would it be too frightening
to reopen the box and see?

All the monsters, I recall.
We loved to glow in the dark,
as we kissed along the wall,
and late at night in the park.
Though, I know, different we felt…

It was just a game, for one.
I never knew how to say…
I hoped the day would be won,
Imagining every way
to continue being held…

But if you sought light from we,
would you have invited me
for a spell to catch lightning,
and would you even like me?

Would the grandeur of the night be
everything we thought it might seem?
Would we spark the flames, finally,
or would we stay, rightly, in dream?

Forever. Untouched by time. You and me.

CHAPTER TWO: LIBERATION

"PARABOLIC HAIKU"

Swiftly the summer breeze warms and cools,
fleeting with the folly of fools.
Freely youth flees its confines,
squandering precious time
on candy and wine,
as sad adults
in clad cults,
in kind,
STOP.
Rewind,
and exult
youthful result,
sipping the divine,
forever in its prime,
reliving between the lines
of our adolescence's schools,
letting kids be kids. Free, and unruled.

"RESOLUTIONS"

The colored lights have all turned off.
The ball has dropped over Times Square,
as we rest in our hotel loft.
New Year's sunlight kisses your hair.
I think back on how we got there…

Three short years stretched toward new life,
shedding vices, shedding tears,
loving views, loving a new wife,
dropping beats, and "'tudes," dropping fears
to the sounds of New Year's cheers…

I'll write books, you'll go back to school,
we'll dance on beaches of the Bay.
I'll wear strange looks, as you stay cool.
We'll both let love win each day,
not worrying if we should stay…

You'll meet new friends, I'll dream new scenes,
we'll both make new memories.
You'll tie loose ends, I'll stream more things.
We'll rewrite our failed histories
into vast, opportune quarries…

The theater lights have all turned on,
and it's time to take center stage.
No matter our choices, we've won
every bet we choose to wage.
We can put any dream to page…

As you rest upon my chest
in sweet, happy reverie,
I can't help but feel we've been blessed.
Hopeful light swells deep inside me.
Life's full of possibilities.

"HOPE"

Hope is the first ray at dawn,
breaking over clouded peaks,
bringing warmth to frigid faun,
loving peace to each who seeks
refuge from unyielding squalls…

Hope is the enduring coal,
lighting obscured path and mind,
fed by heart's belief, in whole,
that miracles we will find
should we break through the dark walls…

Hope brings will, and with it, strength,
like summer breeze filling sail,
to out-traverse any length,
overcome each deadly gaol
wrought by swelling storm's cruel thralls…

Hope defies reason and cage,
filling voids in we who grieve,
quelling night's unending rage,
should we but choose to believe
in the light within us all.

"BE BEAUX"

Locked in a box.
He's still locked in his box,
wasting away like his time.
Wish he would take down his sign.

Thousands of clocks.
He's got thousands of clocks.
Each one is set to go off
every time that we scoff.

He was scarred
by the world,
and now he has just given up.

He was marred
by that girl,
who wanted him to liven up…

Sitting in dirt.
He's just sitting in dirt,
staring at an empty book
with overly delighted looks.

Chugging blue pills.
He's just chugging blue pills,
constantly praying for the end.
Why couldn't he just blend in?

He was barred
from his life
for an extremely dumb mistake.

He had sparred,
without knife,
against that venomous snake.

Go home.
Get out.
Leave with all of your forked tongues.

Stop turning my gold into your dung.
Don't come.
Don't shout.
Close the door, just leave me in peace.
How am I to work on this piece?

Signing a map.
I am designing a map,
one that leads away from here,
and all of the poison I hear.

Ringing a friend.
I am bringing a friend,
one who knows how to lift me up,
one who shows how to gift my love.

In this place
of a sham,
be who you were meant to be.

See my face,

who I am,

not who you want me to be.

There's no race.

I'm not damned.

Why can't all of you just be—

Beaux?

"THIRTEEN"

Thirteen weeks have gone by,
since you last went away.
I look to the night sky,
to the moon, softly pray,
for your safe return…

Thirteen thousand paces
I have fretfully made,
heart skipping beats. It braces,
as if pierced by apt blade,
for the day it's my turn…

Thirteen million bright stars
search for you overhead,
wondering where you are,
where you must make your bed.
Thinking of you, they burn…

Thirteen months have drudged on,
last as dark as the first.
You can't really be gone,
gone off to fight the worst
war— my stomach still churns…

Thirteen boxes I've read,
of letters I have sent—
dreams I wish I had said,
to tell you what you meant,
what you were meant to learn…

Thirteen constellations,
guarding your perfect heart,
deprived of elation.
Wishing I'd played my part,
to save you from this urn…

Thirteen years I have known.
Still, I can't let you go.

"JUST BREATHE"

Breathe. Just breathe.
Listen to the sound of my voice.
Though the world simmers and seethes,
drown out the cerebral noise.
Focus instead,
not on the thoughts in your head,
but the beating in your chest.
Forget all the rest,
or be left for dead.

See. Just see.
Look through the darkness for my light.
In green growing fields, come find me.
Let your soul's glow be your true sight.
Keep fears at bay.
When demons and monsters bar ways,
face them and fight til the end.
Let not your will or resolve bend.
Come what may.

As you hustle and bustle and rustle through leaves,
winding and grinding and blinding your view,
hear your heart—it's a part of the start of you.
Let it guide, not subside, with pure light, on your sleeve.
It revives you, anew.

Now, STOP. I plea.

On your face, feel the wind and rain.
Walk three paces into the clear.
Pain drains, never to come again.
You are safe here.
Rises the dawn with gentle glow,
revealing pathways yet unknown.
Gale and tide, hail and flame, grow calm.
Thunder, shadow give way to psalm,
as our warmth radiates and grows.

Infinitely.

"CITY THAT CARE FORGOT"

For Luis and Les

Step One. Step Two.
Turn. Glance.
Step Three. Step Four.
Shimmy. Spin. Dance.

Spin. Click. Whirr. Twirl.
Bump. Beat.
Mix. Level. Boys. Girls.
Cue. Happy Feet.

In the city that never stops,
where the tracks never skip a beat,
both old and young dance in the streets,
entranced by rainbow-chalked raindrops.
They twizz and whirl, locking their pops,
as they skip and hop, dip and meet,
while spin-masters rally and greet,

tallying amps, cranking their knobs…

Half-step. Full staff.
Blow. Bleat.
In staccato.
Hammering E.

Trumpets trump.
Vibratos in C.
Snares ensnare.
Keyboards change key.

In the city that never sleeps,
where the melodies play all night,
"las bandas" play, rumble and fight,
stumbling as they take flights of cheap
shots from matrons of each other's keeps—
much to the patrons' delight,
who cheer and shout at the sight,
as mics whistle while guitars weep…

One dip. Dot two.
Swish. Stroke.

Long three.Four short.
Brush. Baroque.

Mix and swirl.
Point and splat.
Quaint in orange-red.
Paint it all black.

In the city that's never dull,
where writers write what poets dream,
and artists' art wows the streams
of streaming 'Tokkers' in The Gulf,
though low tides slow and lull,
eager eyes gleam and wide smiles beam,
in this city of high esteem—
It's here I'll rest my seasoned scull.

CHAPTER THREE: BEAUTY

"BEAUTY"

Fit, stylishly dressed.
Hair fragrantly fine.
Face vibrantly refreshed,
as you sip on divine wine.

Skin smooth and sun-kissed.
Lips sweet as honey.
Watching, in heavenly bliss,
starry eyes twinkling at me.

Bodily perfect, I find…
More enticing, still— your mind.

Your thoughts.
Your soul.
Curiosity.
Wonderment.
Your views.
Kindness.

Passion.

Your heart.

Like diamonds hidden from view,
with crystal clarity,
of varying hues,
mind, soul, and body—
perfect, pure and true—
entrusted tenderly,
as we vow, "I do."
For it is your heart's beauty
I love most about you.

Affectionately.

Earnestly.

In perpetuity.

"6AM"

Sweetly does she shine,
Great Herald of the morn.
Faithful to the divine,
doting to the forlorn
sympathetic kindness,
inspiring mindfulness
to remind, with each storm
Mother Dawn gives her warmth.

"FIRE AND LIGHTNING"

I see you,
looking from across the bar.
Skull and poisoned dagger
stitched across your heart.
With a man, looking like you'd rather
hop in this storm and fly real far,
basking in the moonlight, lathered
in the twinkles of a thousand stars…

I need you,
like thunder needs lightning.
Three parts wild and untamed,
two parts loud, but exciting,
like a category yet unnamed,
riding bucking wind, frightening
the timid hiding in their enclave,
shaking at the first sighting…

Your touch will thrill.
Your kiss will kill.
Your looks chill, but still,
I'm addicted to your energy.

Your gaze will burn.
My world will churn.
Your every word
incinerates with intensity.

I read you.
We're on the crowded dance floor,
wrapping legs and arms around mine,
as the locals head for the door.
The rhythm of our moves combine,
swiftly knocking people on fours.
Our hearts form a nuclear mine.
Our lips create a firestorm…

I lead you--
every turn and spin--
each snapping thrust and kick.
Our feet command the wind.
When we shuffle quick,
we draw everyone in,
lighting oiled wicks
with increasingly greased lightning...

You flash, I crack.
You spark, step back.
Char it all to black.
The skies roar and rumble.

The wild gales wail.
It storms and hails.
As nonstop we assail
with blasts. The earth crumbles.

I plead you,
when the music calms and stops

and our dance comes to an end,

not to disappear or drop

my beating heart as you ascend

the rainclouds, back atop

the heavens with your boyfriend.

You just smile and fade into the backdrop.

"MY DANDELION"

Your love is a dandelion.

Sunny and bright,

filled with healing light.

Hopeful and carefree,

carried on a melodic breeze…

Your smile is a fine wine.

Enticing and bold,

spicy, even when cold.

Yet, never too much,

and always warm when our lips touch…

Your eyes are like great scions

to vast cosmic skies,

each twinkling spark wise,

profoundly primed,

beyond e'en a thousand lifetimes…

Your heart is the Rhine.

Boundlessly free,

untethered to creed.

Grand on any chart,

and, of course, my favorite part…

Happy, I am, that you are mine…

for all time.

"THINGS I ~~HATE~~ ~~MISS~~ *LOVE* ABOUT YOU"

You come waltzing home
with a smug look on your face,
like you just won the whole place
But can't be bugged to answer your phone…
You'd complain how cramped it was,
how there wasn't space for your crown,
cursing when stuff came falling down
Yet your things made the walls bust…

But those puppy eyes
got me every time
I'd take you back
like chocolate crack

We'd kiss with such fury,
making love in a hurricane,
like it was the end
and we were just 'round the bend…

You would often disappear
for several days at a time,
then send me to the back of line
and have the nerve to demand a beer
You would make me so mad
We would yell and scream, I'd cry,
waking neighbors when things would fly
You'd storm off, I'd feign I was glad…

But those big brown eyes
melt me every time
I'd let you back,
forgive what you lacked

Our kisses blew the room
like love in a monsoon
The dark skies would part,
as lightning struck my worn out heart…

I woke up all alone,

wondering where you could be

I said mean things I didn't mean

'til you were finally... gone

Now I mull and I mope

in this empty kingdom of one,

loathing everything I'd done,

feeling I destroyed every hope...

I miss those happy eyes

warming me each time

You'd laugh for a while

with that silly smile

Running fingers through hair

Drawing hearts everywhere,

head resting on your chest,

knowing with you was where I fit best...

I trudge through each lonely day

in arid heat, but feeling cold,

wanting only you to hold
Wishing you'd come back some way
As I lie beneath a blackened moon
listening to the sullen stars,
thinking about kissing in your car,
while the speakers play our tune…

You sneak in with those eyes
that could tell no lies,
slipping your hand in mine,
speaking everything is fine

Swiftly, I hold you tight
Never gonna say goodbye
to this rare love we grew
from things I ~~hate~~ *~~miss~~* **LOVE** about you

"FOREVER NEAR"

When the winds of change
blow fiercely upon you
and the masks rearrange
to obscure scars from view…

When the frosted halls
Slowly begin to melt
and your sculptured walls
reveal the traumas felt…

When you pull away
quickly to survive
apocalyptic shame,
know you don't have to hide.

Each burn is a tale
of interwoven strength
overcoming past fails,
enduring pain at length.

Each crack in the ice
is a well-earned place
for your resplendent light
to unmask your lovely face.

Each time that you feel
alone in the dark
in an unending wheel
with demons grim and stark…

Hold my warm hands.
Recall if you can.
Look into my eyes.
Break thru the lies.
Hear my beating heart.
Play your true part.
Like you were meant to.
I still live for you.

So, sing every song.
Let your beauty show,

knowing I am here.

Forever near.

CHAPTER FOUR: IMAGINATION

"ANEW"

Melodic sons rise
Ribbons of rhythmic rays
permeate and perpetuate
good feels of this day,
opening hearts and eyes...

Raindrop drums beat
upon pondering ponds,
unlocking ten thousand gates
to the great beyond,
each one dropping ten thousand feet...

Legato winds blow,
connecting minds and souls
to free their floundering fates
from their shipwrecked shoals,
restoring their natural flow...

Winged strings sing for you,
telling tall, telling tales—
hours of our fifty first dates
traversing untrodden trails—
as this day loves, anew.

"RIVER OF SOUND"

I float upon a river of sound,
carried by beats of percussive drums,
flowing free, without borders or bounds,
streamed in seams of picking and sly strums.
Melodically.

I dote upon a river of sound,
enraptured by its pervasive tides,
as it grows, weaves and compounds.
Crescendos like rollercoaster rides.
Emphatically.

I float upon a river of sound,
made of interwoven strings of gold,
rising and falling with each pounding
of my speakers' heart, spry dreams untold.
Harmoniously.

I wrote upon this river of sound,
with a pulsing pen of sines, cosines,
frequencies frequently loud and proud.

Turning heads.
Waking dead.
Mixing finds.
Bending minds.

Notes in tune,
waves of 'Moon(light)
Sonata,' and
'Toccata,'
iN. sTo. CcA. tO.
*with **BRAVADO**,*
immune to blight,
and out of sight,

Pumping bass, as I vibrate in time.
Rhythmically.

"READY FOR YOU"

Each and every night,
I wait beneath this sky,
wondering which bright star
brings me to where you are.

I dream of pale moonlight
kissing your silky hair.
Firelight dances in your eyes,
never saying goodbye.

A soft whisper takes flight,
your sweet lips at my ear,
confessing, "I love you."
I've always loved you, too.

Oh, how I wish I might
feel your heart beat with mine
in synched, symphonic streams
outside these fleeting dreams.

Though we haven't met— not quite,
and dreams may sour or fade,
to be loved in return
would be worth the pained burn.

So, as these hopes shine bright,
beneath this starlit sea,
my heart yearns, just in view,
waiting, and ready for you.

"UPON A CLOUD"

Listless, I waft upon a cloud.
Dream, caught in unending nightmare.
Seemingly afraid to speak loud.
Wishless, without a single care,
screaming silence in stagnant air.

Too dangerous it is to hope.
Daylight burns the feeble fancy.
Midnight waits to stifle and choke
blue skies of dreams wild and carefree,
true lies lying waste to reverie.

And yet, eternally burn flames
of passion for rising above
dispassion brought by winds of change.
And bet upon conquering love.
Not ashen will be dreams hereof.

Blissful, I float upon a cloud,

silvery lining as my bed.

Still very shiny, new, and proud.

Wishful, without a sense of dread,

dreams flowing in streams from my head.

"MY FANTASY"

It's a mid-autumn Saturday.
Our leaves have begun to change.
It even feels a little strange,
but as I think on what to say,
for once, I know it'll be fine…

As I write out your birthday card,
unaware of your devilish smile,
you spin me around for a while.
We fall down and both laugh so hard—
this dreamy fantasy of mine.

A secret path catches my eye,
and the sound of a nearby band.
You wink, grabbing both of my hands,
leading me behind the ivy,
as we try the Electric Slide.

Though we have four confused left feet,
you say you love me anyways,
and we dance for what seems like days,
until our lips finally meet,
tasting of 'bubble-berry' wine.

After the very last slow dance,
we start to walk back, in the cold.
You kiss my head, and closely hold
my heart in your weathering hands,
as I fall asleep on the ride

Home.

Not wanting to awaken me,
you lie me on snow lily beds,
again kissing my 'sleepy head,'
safe in sweetly wandering dreams—
evergreen, like whispering pines.

When I wake to the dawn's warm light,

and the dream long came to an end,

you greet me like a long-lost friend.

Everything's gonna be alright—

you stayed—and not just in my mind.

You, alone.

"WINTER LOVE, IN STILL-FRAME"

Colored lights slowly twinkle
in the quiet world below.
The scent of pines evergreen
mixes with fresh floating snow,
which glistens as it sprinkles
us with a soft, gentle glow
on a breeze pure and pristine,
like kisses sweetly grown…

Alpine air carries wind chimes,
like confessions of true love.
We listen to winter hymns sublime
from snowcapped hills up above,
in this moment frozen in time.
Nestled like two turtle doves,
atop the crest of a long climb,
we craft diamonds from the rough…

Beneath magical starlight,
you rest your weary head.
Every moment feels right
as you slumber on my beating chest.
I wish with all of my might,
choosing to cherish this instead,
that forever lasts this night,
just holding you close to breast,

In love's unending light.

CHAPTER FIVE: TRUE LOVE

"HAPPY VALENTINES"

Even if I had money
or power or wishes two,
I would still want to make
all your biggest dreams come true.
But til that day comes, see
five things I love about you.

I love the way you smile.
How it brightens any room.

I love your inner child.
How he's not afraid to bloom.

I love how you get wild
whenever we're on Zoom™.

I love you stay a while
when most avoid the gloom.

But the thing I love most
amongst all your virtues
is the truth in your eyes
that says you love me too.
Though wealth I've little to boast,
I'm thankful each day for you.

Happy Valentines

"CLUMSY LOVE"

I see you walk by every day.
The sunlight brightens your way.
Melodies sing when you stop to say,
"One coffee. No cream."

Your smile makes me feel so weak.
My heart can't help but spring a leak
every time I hear you speak.
I start to daydream…

Gray eyes twinkle at me.
Fingers run through my hair.
My cheeks blush when I see
just how much you care
as you get on one knee
to tighten your loose shoe…

When our hands briefly touch, I fall
in love with how sweetly appalled

you look as I spill it all
over your favorite boots…

Terrified, I just want to die,
but you smile with those soothing eyes,
softly whispering that I
am crushing your foot…

But when I clean the mess,
you pull me in close,
holding me to confess
I'm the one you need the most,
of everyone I could guess,
to be your forever boo

And amazingly just like this,
you lean in without remissness,
as we share our very first kiss,
while angels sing from up above…

For the first time, it all feels right,

as you warm me with gentle light.

Then you ask to see me tonight.

My heart explodes with clumsy love!

"INDEPENDENCE DAY"

T'was like a midsummer night's dream.
The kind hotter than it should be.
Something boring was on the stream
at a friend's holiday party.
You walked in so very late,
with so very much on your plate—
disheveled hair, and loosened tie,
specks of mischief in your eye...

During some long-winded speech,
as our bubbles came into view,
you sat down just across from me,
catching me daydreaming of you.
You smiled and motioned outside.
Something about Bonnie and Clyde.
You were mouthing for me to wait
at some time after half-passed eight...

Then the lights went out.
People yelled and shout,
as hands flailed about.
Yours found mine.

You whispered to me
if I wanted to be
a little crazy.
I said fine.

While they still stumbled in the dark,
you led me out on the deck,
singing like a drunken lark,
to the edge of the old shipwreck.
We stepped to the pier's end and
you held my shivering hands,
closed my eyes, asked me to trust you,
then into the water we flew!

Somewhere in the brine,
your soft lips met mine.

At exactly nine
were loud pops.

There above the sea,
where you embraced me,
fireworks kissed like we.
Never to stop.

"ROLLERCOASTER"

You say I'm needy—
rules from ceiling to floor.
Puritan in a seedy
bar the windows and door.

I say you're petty—
pushing buttons 'til they break.
Just like Bea, and Betty
White stripes at a black-tie wake.

"Take it back," you cry.
Our things start to fly,
as I head outside,
and out of your life.
Then, you call my phone.
We both feel alone,
so you hold me close,
and we overdose…

…on love.

You say I'm too neat—
everything in its place,
like some kinda deity
'ex machina' to save face.

I say you're too pretty—
stylishly wild and raw,
like some kind of prized kitty,
tabled with middle-fingered paw.

I'm judgy, you say.
I blurt you're fake.
You quip, "Run and play."
I call you names.
You slam the door.
I miss you more.
We both cry on the floor,
as we implore…

…for love.

You say you need me
more with each passing day,
dying, unable to breathe
life into you, to feel okay.

I say I've felt itty
bitty in a big world,
grayed without love, or pity
fools of sorrow in fetal curls.

You say I'm missed
I say I'm not pissed.
You lean in to kiss.
We can fix this.
You break down my walls.
I blush, enthralled.
We slow dance in the hall,
as again we fall…

...in love.

"BLUE ROSE"

A blue Rose lies on a swath
of stained cordovan,
rigid and lifeless,
buried beneath sand,
searingly cold, like nature's wrath.

Melancholy Moonlight
plays somberly overhead,
stifled only by ocean roars.
Somewhere deep in regret,
a man drowns out of sight.

Had he only answered the call.
Had they not had that squall.
Had she not run from it all
to escape in the light of the moon,
plunging deep with needle and spoon…

But now she's gone,
beyond truth and reason.
Never again will he see
his sweet Rose by the sea,
seeing starlight twinkling
gleefully between
marred blights from galaxies
stowed in the windows to her soul.

"HALF EMPTY"

I lie beneath an empty sky,
reeking of cheap cigarettes,
our distance in close vignette.
A void overhead, as inside.

Somewhere, your day has just begun.
Some people say to just be through.
Somehow, I keep missing you.
I could never say that we're done.

A knife twists every night
I go to sleep alone. I rain,
doubting when I'll see you again,
wishing for a little of your light…

Every time I think of you,
my heart weakens and breaks in two.
I suffocate.
Hyperventilate.

I can't escape
the sounds of my own tears.

I need to hear your voice,
drown out all of this noise—
thoughts in my head,
words you said,
rather be dead
than confirm my worst fears…

I lie beneath half-empty skies,
seeking frets from long ago.
Symphonic chorus to a song
we both knew all along just why

You always light up my life.

"THE ONLY ONE"

For Charlie

I am thankful for the presents,
the well-wishes and good cheer.
Cards and cocoa may keep me warm,
but one thing's still missing this year.
As the snow falls this holiday,
and bright laughter fills our ears,
I just wish this will come true—
The only one I need is you…

I would give up everything—
from snow angels to the stars
I would give up the best trees,
snickerdoodle cookies in jars.
I'd even give up caroling
by people both near and far,
because just one thing I could choose—
Bae, only one I need is you…

Lights and candles may brighten skies.
Spinning dreidels may widen eyes.
Chocolate coins may widen smiles,
but without you, my blues compile.

I would give up garlands of chrome
building men made of fresh snow,
I would give up gingerbread homes,
and each good year to come, you know.
I'd even give up trips to Rome,
to see you 'neath the mistletoe.
This one dream, please make it come true—
The only one I need is you.

My sweet Bae, just say you'll do—
The only one I need— is you.

"LIFE'S GRAIL"

I have played the wise sage.
I have stayed many duels.
Even prayed away plagues,
but I am just a fool
each time I see you smile…

I have been wide and far.
I have seen diamond sands.
Even gleaned every star,
but when I hold your hands,
my heart stutters, beguiled.

Your eyes enchant.
Ears, confidants.
Your voice descants
of love across lifetimes…

Your humor charms.
Apt wit disarms.

Kind soul e'er warms
these lonely rimes…

Thousands have fought for you.
Hundreds have brought tributes.
Their flames grow hot, it's true,
enamored, dazed, confused,
for inklings of your love.

Choose, why then, little me,
last of the middle three,
who's crumbling brittlely,
fast falling, immotilely,
'fore life's grail from above?

Your love's a gift—
rising, it lifts
spirits which drift—
present for few…

Though don't know why
you set your eyes,
thankful am I,
each day with you.

"SHAWNEE PROVERB"

"So live your life that the fear of death can never enter your heart."

Tecumseh

Acknowledgements

Special thanks to all the people who inspired, encouraged, promoted and believed in me, including but not limited to my husband, my friends, family, my second-year college English teacher, and of course, you the readers. Without all of you, I may never have put words to paper.

So, thank you. From the bottom of my heart.

www.ingramcontent.com/pod-product-compliance
Lightning Source LLC
LaVergne TN
LVHW041617070526
838199LV00052B/3178